© Bruce A. Fletcher Oct. 2008

ACTS Ministries Inte:

106 South St

West Hartford, CT 06110

bccwh.org

1st Printing Feb. 2009

All rights reserved under International Copyright Law. Contents and or cover may not be reproduced in whole or in part in any form without the express written consent of the author/publisher. Unless otherwise indicated, all Scriptures are from *The New King James Version.* Nashville: Thomas Nelson, 1982

1st Revision June 2020

I want to thank my wife Lisa for her undying support and encouragement to pursue God's plan for my life. Without her support, I would not be where I am today. Because of that, I dedicate this book to her.

May God richly bless you!

Contents

Foreword 5
1. Standing for Success 7
   Seated With Christ 8
   Walking in Newness of Character 11
   Standing in the Battle 12
2. Different Levels of Maturity 15
   Sacrificial Living 16
   Am I My Brother's Keeper? 17
   Look Out For Each Other 19
3. Two of the Greatest Enemies 22
   Complacency 22
   Asleep in America 23
   Mediocrity 24
   The Second Mile Club 26
4. Stand on the Wall 30
   Who Is Responsible? 31
   Testing Prophecy 33
5. Defense Wins Championships 36

    Be Proactive 37

    Live to Win 40

6. Be Strong in the Lord 42

    Our Strength is in the Lord 43

    Resisting Evil 44

    Face Challenges and Embrace Them 46

7. Our Responsibility 49

    Faith is not in Vain 50

    Abounding in the Work of the Lord 51

    Don't Waver 52

8. Finish What You Start 55

    Time to Sprint 56

    A Warning from Paul 57

9. Stand Firm; Stand Fast 60

    Where Will You Be After the Smoke Has Cleared? . 61

    Casting our Crowns 62

    There's More to Come 63

    Learn to Stand Under Pressure 63

    The True Strength of a Preacher 65

Foreword

There is a saying that I hear frequently; "If you don't stand for something, you'll fall for anything." While it may be a slight exaggeration, there is a strong element of truth to it.

In relation to the Kingdom of God and His righteousness, it's time for Christians to stand up and be counted. By taking a stand, we will shine the Light of Truth upon the kingdom of darkness, exposing the lies and deceit that are holding so many people captive.

The first step in spiritual victory is to secure a position in which you are standing strong in the Lord. May the Lord strengthen and enable you for the battles that lie ahead.

1. **Standing for Success**

Ephesians 6:10-13 (NKJV) [10] Finally, my brethren, be strong in the Lord and in the power of His might. [11] Put on the whole armor of God that you may be able to stand against the wiles of the devil. [12] for we do not wrestle against flesh and blood, but against principalities, against powers, against the rulers of the darkness of this age, against spiritual hosts of wickedness in the heavenly places. [13] Therefore take up the whole armor of God that you may be able to withstand in the evil day, and having done all, to stand.

We need to learn how to stand if we are going to be successful. Success is not measured by accumulated wealth or even by past experiences. True success is when you have done everything that you know to do and need to do, then you take a stand and don't lose it all because of thoughtlessness and lightheartedness.

The book of Ephesians is a letter from the Apostle Paul that has answers to the questions we have about standing strong and gaining victory through spiritual warfare. The letter can easily be divided into three parts based upon three principles that Paul teaches. The three principles are each expressed by single words: Sit, Walk, Stand. These three principles are also sequential.

Seated With Christ

(Ephesians 2:4-7 NKJV) [4] But God, who is rich in mercy, because of His great love with which He loved us, [5] even when we were dead in trespasses, made us alive together with Christ (by grace you have been saved), [6] and raised us up together, and made us sit together in the heavenly places in Christ Jesus, [7] that in the ages to come He might show the exceeding riches of His grace in His kindness toward us in Christ Jesus.

It is critical to understand that where you have been seated has determined how you are walking; how you are walking determined the stand you currently are taking.

The Bible uses sitting frequently as a metaphor representing association. One example is:

> Psalm 1:1 (NKJV) Blessed *is* the man Who walks not in the counsel of the ungodly, Nor stands in the path of sinners, Nor sits in the seat of the scornful;

As Paul reveals, Christ is seated far above all principalities and powers. Now, we are seated with Him in a position of power over the evil forces of darkness. This is a spiritual position that must be realized by all believers. We are placed in a position of power here on the earth because of our new standing with God.

To help you understand what it means to be seated with Christ, I want to use the example of a National President or the King of an Empire. Even though their office, such as the Oval Office at the White House, represents their power, they don't have to be in that room to exercise their power. No matter where they are within their nation or kingdom, they have the power associated with their office.

It is that way with Jesus' body, His Church in the earth. We are designated by Him to represent Him here in the earth. Because we are seated with Him, we have authority anywhere we are in the world. Our authority is over His enemies, the principalities and powers of darkness. You do not have to be physically present in Heaven to have Heaven's power and authority.

From this elevated seat, we fight from the position of victory, not defeat. We are given victory before the battle even begins. This is a present reality that must be received by and lived out through faith. Having this perspective will change your attitude under pressure.

In essence, the Christian is already delivered from the dominion of darkness. Sin and Satan no longer have power over them.

Instead of being dominated, Christian's should exert dominance over both Sin and Satan.

Walking in Newness of Character

Ephesians 4:1-3 (NKJV) [1] I, therefore, the prisoner of the Lord, beseech you to walk worthy of the calling with which you were called, [2] with all lowliness and gentleness, with longsuffering, bearing with one another in love, [3] endeavoring to keep the unity of the Spirit in the bond of peace.

The second section deals with walking out the character of Christ in the earth. We no longer walk as unsaved people. Therefore, we must manifest the characteristics of this new life in Christ. Harmonize your conduct with your calling. Know who you are in Christ and live in that manner at all times. In the context of this passage, our calling is to walk in unity with fellow believers.

Walking out Christ's character is how we manifest His presence to the earth. If we believe that He has conquered sin, death and the grave, we then need to manifest it in our character.

In order to stand in the face of adversity and not shrink back, we first have to realize our position in Christ, walk as He did, and then, take a bold stand.

Knowing the first two principles is essential to having the boldness and confidence necessary to be victorious over every trial and temptation we are facing and will face.

Standing in the Battle

Ephesians 6:10; 13 (NKJV) [10] Finally, my brethren, be strong in the Lord and in the power of His might.

[13] Therefore take up the whole armor of God that you may be able to withstand in the evil day, and having done all, to stand.

This section of Ephesians deals with standing. This will be the focus of this book; Standing Firm.

When I think about standing, I think about trees. I have experienced both hurricanes and tornadoes. After strong winds blow through an area, you can see the devastation it leaves behind. Trees are broken off and some even uprooted.

The tree that receives the most damage is the Southern Pine. They may be tall and large in circumference, but they are a soft wood. They look good, but are not real strong.

However, an oak tree can withstand strong winds. It has an extremely healthy root system as well as being hard. Adversity to the oak actually strengthens it, enabling it to withstand even stronger storms.

Are you an Oak or Pine?

Allow the Lord to strengthen you and strengthen yourself in Him. This involves both seeking and yielding. He will meet you where you are and take you to where He wants you to be.

2. Different Levels of Maturity

There are different levels of maturity in Christianity. With each level comes new understanding as well as responsibility. The four stages are simply, Infancy, Childhood, Adolescence, and then Adulthood. We grow into each one as we are trained and eventually learn to stand on our own two feet. We do not attain to each level according to how long we have been saved. It's not the same as the physical growth. Attainment to maturity comes through willful submission to God and His ways.

One of the signs that a Christian has grown into adulthood is that they are familiar with and use the armor of God as described in Eph. 6. Each of the pieces of armor represents characteristics of Jesus. We must apply these characteristics and principles in order to live a victorious life.

Also, the adult Christian knows what spiritual warfare is and how to engage in it in a Scriptural manner. They know what it takes to win the battle.

I encourage you to examine yourself and see what level of maturity you have attained. Be honest with yourself and be willing to take the necessary steps to grow into the stature of the fullness of Christ.

Ephesians 4:13 (NKJV) [13] till we all come to the unity of the faith and of the knowledge of the Son of God, to a perfect man, to the measure of the stature of the fullness of Christ.

Mature Christians who know how to stand in battle not only for themselves, but also for the benefit of those around them.

Sacrificial Living

Sacrificial living is an essential part of maturity. Selfish people have already put themselves into a position of defeat because they are not open to the needs of others. Selfishness will produce greed and short-sightedness.

In Corinth, the Christian's there were beginning to operate with selfishness in their meetings. There was not just an abuse and misuse of the gifts, they had become selfish in the way they conducted their love feasts. Poor people were being left out while the rich were going overboard. Some were even over-indulging with the wine and becoming drunk. As a result, they were abusing the significance of the Lord's Supper. This resulted in some being sick and many more even dying. Paul had to correct their behavior and get them focused again on brotherly love (1 Cor. 11).

Am I My Brother's Keeper?

Genesis 4:9 (NKJV) ⁹ Then the LORD said to Cain, "Where *is* Abel your brother?" He said, "I do not know. *Am* I my brother's keeper?"

Cain, because of his selfishness, refused to adhere to God's plan for sacrificing. Jealousy set in on him and eventually it produced a murdering spirit in Cain. Consequently, instead of repenting, he murdered his brother and then tried to act like he knew nothing about it.

Cain's problem with anger began when he decided that he would worship and sacrifice the way he wanted to. He created the first man made replacement to true worship. When his brother remained faithful to God's way, Cain would either have to repent or get rid of what was causing him the conviction.

Cain's anger not only caused him to murder his brother, he became angry and indignant with God. When he asked, "Am I my brother's keeper?" he was not asking because he wasn't sure. He was being sarcastic with God. After all, if he was sincere, why did God have to reject his offering?

Have you ever said that it doesn't matter how you worship as long as you worship? Maybe you are one who believes that it doesn't matter how you get to God as long as you get there. It was Jesus that said He was the Way. It's not man's idea; it's Jesus way. God will accept no other way.

Does seeing your Christian Brother or Sister prosper cause anger in you? Or, do you rejoice with them? If you are unable to rejoice with another person who gains blessing, it is a sign of immaturity. How can you stand in battle with someone you are jealous of?

Look Out For Each Other

Ephesians 4:1–3 (NKJV) [11] Deliver those who are drawn toward death, and hold back those stumbling to the slaughter.

1 Corinthians 10:24 (NKJV) [24] Let no one seek his own, but each one the other's well-being.

The thing that is of primary importance for a Christian is the welfare of others. We need to look out for others, especially those that have a hard time caring for themselves. It's easy to help those that we know can pay us back, but what about those that have no way to repay? Should we ignore their needs? Hear what Jesus says:

> "When you give a dinner or a supper, do not ask your friends, your brothers, your relatives, or rich neighbors, lest they also invite you back, and you are repaid. But when you give a feast, invite the poor, *the* maimed, *the* lame, *and the* blind. And you will be blessed, because they cannot repay you; for you shall be repaid at the resurrection of the just." (Lk 14:12-14).

Secondary to that are the Christian's liberties. When we put our rights before the needs of others, we are not walking in maturity.

The consequence of selfishness is inability to stand in our own battles. The enemy has already gained a foothold into our lives through selfishness.

3. Two of the Greatest Enemies

Two of the greatest enemies we face today are complacency and mediocrity.

Complacency

Proverbs 1:32 (NKJV)
³² For the turning away of the simple will slay them, and the complacency of fools will destroy them;

James 4:17 (NKJV)
¹⁷ Therefore, to him who knows to do good and does not do it, to him it is sin.

What is complacency? It is to be self-satisfied and unaware of possible dangers around you. The picture of complacency is an ostrich with its head buried in the sand, not wanting to be bothered by the events going on around it.

Asleep in America

Has the Church fallen asleep? There is a spiritual battle raging around us. Souls are falling daily to drugs, alcohol, and immorality. Yet, the Church is busy building bigger buildings as monuments to themselves. People are living under bridges and eating out of garbage cans while some Christian groups pretend that it's not their problem if it isn't happening at their doorstep.

I know this sounds harsh, but it's time to wake up. Does God want us building multi-million-dollar buildings or His Church?

Complacency has so gripped us that we aren't fully aware of the great battle for souls. Why should Satan be allowed to win when the Church is equipped with every spiritual resource it needs to be victorious?

Between 1725 and 1760, America experienced a period we refer to as the Great Awakening. Men and women were awakened to their depravity and need for God. Communities turned to God in repentance. It was not done through eloquence or personal charisma, but by the Holy Spirit gripping the hearts of preachers and then through them the hearts of the hearers.

Has your heart been gripped by the desperate need you see around you? Does it bother you that the devil seems to be running rampant while most of Christianity is at rest in their pristine palaces? Then rise up and be a voice in the world! Call for repentance and reform in the dead Churches.

It's time for another Great Awakening! Who will be the voice and catalyst for such a movement? Will you?

Mediocrity

Mediocrity is a quality that is adequate or acceptable, but not very good. It's enough to get by.

Recently I had a student who was taking a quiz in History and Geography. We required him to get an 80% or better in order to move on. I looked at the final score and he had an 82%. I decided to look at the quiz to see what he missed. He had actually skipped important questions that were too difficult for him. He calculated what he needed to pass, and that's all that he did.

When I questioned him about it, he said, "I passed. That is all that matters, right?" As you can imagine, I took the opportunity to address mediocrity in his studies. If we don't change the mindset of children now, what do you think they'll be like when they become adults?

The opposite of mediocrity is excellence. How many times have you been involved in a ministry or Church event that was well planned but poorly executed? It seems that sometimes people feel that because they are volunteers, they don't have to work hard. I have heard people remark that you can't expect more if they aren't being paid. Who are they working for anyway?

> *Colossians 3:17 (NKJV) [17] And whatever you do in word or deed, do all in the name of the Lord Jesus, giving thanks to God the Father through Him.*

Do you want to offer God sloppy, half-hearted work? I don't think so.

We repel people by being half-hearted. If your whole heart is not in your relationship with God, why would anyone want to listen to you and surrender their lives to Christ?

The Second Mile Club

Matthew 5:41 (NKJV)

[41] And whoever compels you to go one mile, go with him two.

Again, the definition of mediocrity is doing just enough to get by. Jesus blew that theory out of the water by telling His disciples to go beyond what was expected or demanded of them.

If they were forced to carry a soldier's equipment for one mile as Roman law allowed, He told them to continue on the second mile. At that point, you are going beyond what is required or customary. No longer are you under the control of the Roman law, you are now going beyond the expectation of the law.

What kind of person are you? Do you go the first mile, grumbling and complaining all the way or do you do it with love and joy?

Think about how much better your Church, home, school, or even your workplace would be if everyone did what was required and then some. I would probably have to pinch myself if one of my children said that they not only cleaned their room, but they also mowed the lawn and took out the garbage!

The person that is a second mile person is the one whom God will bring greater blessing to. There is a level of work and conduct that is expected just because we are Christian's. Then, there is the level that goes beyond showing the love and character of God in a dynamic manner. Consider the following verse about God:

> *Ephesians 3:20-21 (NKJV) [20] Now to Him who is able to do exceedingly abundantly above all that we ask or think, according to the power that works in us, [21] to Him be glory in the church by Christ Jesus to all generations, forever and ever. Amen.*

Do you want the exceeding, abundant provision of God, or do you want just enough of His blessing in your life to get by? Remember, the outflow is a part of the overflow. You give out of the abundance God pours into your life. If $10.00 buys a meal, then $20.00 will buy one for you and someone else. You are able to be used by God to bless people in need because you live in the overflow.

Mediocrity demands that it's only about you and no one else. Break out of the cycle of mediocrity today. Join the "Second Mile Club!"

4. Stand on the Wall

Isaiah 62:6 (NKJV) ⁶ I have set watchmen on your walls, O Jerusalem; they shall never hold their peace day or night. You who make mention of the LORD, do not keep silent

There is a need to have mature men and women taking a stand as watchmen. A watchman is one who is looking out from a higher vantage point than everyone else; they have a distinct advantage in that they can see further and more clearly.

However, with this position comes a greater responsibility. God gave a warning to both watchman and people:

Ezekiel 33:3-6 (NKJV) ³ when he sees the sword coming upon the land, if he blows the trumpet and warns the people, ⁴ then whoever hears the sound of the trumpet and does not take warning, if the sword comes and takes him away, his blood shall be on his own head. ⁵ He heard the sound of the trumpet, but did not take warning; his blood shall be upon himself. But he who takes warning will save his life. ⁶ But if the watchman sees the sword coming and does not blow the trumpet, and the people are not warned, and the sword comes and takes any person from among them, he is taken away in his iniquity; but his blood I will require at the watchman's hand.'

Who Is Responsible?

Here, responsibilities are clearly defined. Fist, the watchman is to blow the warning trumpet if there is danger coming. If the people respond, they will be saved; if they don't, they are personally responsible for their own destruction.

On the other hand, if the watchman failed to sound a warning and disaster struck, then the watchman was responsible for the destruction.

The question arises for every believer: For whom will God hold us responsible? To whom shall we witness? Whom shall we warn? We can start with our relatives, fellow workers, neighbors and friends. "It is a solemn responsibility, and we do harm to our own soul if we do not fulfill it faithfully.[1]"

Ezekiel was called by God to be a watchman. He was given a ministry that would most likely have very few people who would heed his warning.

There is an appearance of glamour associated with the prophetic ministry. Modern day Pentecostals and Charismatic's have in many ways distorted the importance of the prophetic ministry. They love to give "Words" that tell everyone that "all is well. God is so pleased with us because we are His children." When, in fact, there may be rampant sin and rebellion surrounding them. A true watchman sees the danger and sounds an alarm in a way that brings people to repentance unto God. They don't have to do

---

[1] William MacDonald and Arthur Farstad, *Believer's Bible Commentary: Old and New Testaments*, Ezek 33:1 (Nashville: Thomas Nelson, 1997, c1995).

it in a mean, sarcastic way as if they were already in heaven and the rest of us are still here on earth.

Testing Prophecy

So, when you receive a prophetic word, how do you know if it's true? You must test the spirits and the prophet. Do they have true godly character when they aren't prophesying? Do they give glory to God through their message and life? Does their word contradict the written word? Are they sarcastic and arrogant or kind and humble?

Jesus told us how to recognize true and false prophets:

> Matthew 7:15–20 (NKJV) 15 "Beware of false prophets, who come to you in sheep's clothing, but inwardly they are ravenous wolves. 16 You will know them by their fruits. Do men gather grapes from thorn bushes or figs from thistles? 17 Even so, every good tree bears good fruit, but a bad tree bears bad fruit. 18 A good tree cannot bear bad fruit, nor *can* a bad tree bear good fruit. 19 Every

tree that does not bear good fruit is cut down and thrown into the fire.

[20] Therefore by their fruits you will know them.

There are seasoned, proven prophets in the Church today. Also, there are new prophets on the rise. They are receiving dreams and visions from God. In humility, they are submitting these to their leaders to be judged and interpreted before they are shared. They seek glory for God and not themselves.

The Apostle Paul wrote:

> 1 Corinthians 14:29 (NKJV) Let two or three prophets speak, and let the others judge.

The Church needs to recognize and accept the prophetic watchmen who are taking a stand on the walls of our lives. They are willing to risk all for the sake of the call. Hear the voice of God through the prophetic ministry and take heed to your souls.

5. Defense Wins Championships

1 Peter 5:8-9 (NLT) [8] Stay alert! Watch out for your great enemy, the devil. He prowls around like a roaring lion, looking for someone to devour. [9] Stand firm against him, and be strong in your faith. Remember that your Christian brothers and sisters all over the world are going through the same kind of suffering you are. [2]

In the sports world, many football enthusiasts cry out that defense wins championships. There is some truth to that, but without offense, you are hard pressed to score touchdowns. On occasion the defense will score, but the chances are greater that your offense will have to step up.

In warfare, you need both offense and defense. Not only do Christian's need to defend themselves against attacks and temptations, they must also mount an offensive against them.

---

[2] Tyndale House Publishers. *Holy Bible: New Living Translation.* 2nd ed. Wheaton, Ill.: Tyndale House Publishers, 2004.

Be Proactive

The Proverb's offer advice on being proactive:

> Proverbs 22:3 (NKJV) "A prudent *man* foresees evil and hides himself, But the simple pass on and are punished."
>
> Proverbs 22:3 (NLT) "A prudent person foresees danger and takes precautions. The simpleton goes blindly on and suffers the consequences."

Most people tend to be reactive rather than proactive. Because of this, instead of gaining ground in their spiritual lives, they are working to maintain and survive.

In the devotional, *Connect the Testaments: A One-Year Daily Devotional with Bible Reading Plan,* we read:

> "Too often we allow ourselves to live passively. We enter into situations without thinking things through or recognizing that we're about to be hurt by others. Yet we as Christians are at war against the evil in the world—not

just against people, but also the unseen forces of evil (Eph 6:12). When we feel oppression, we must resist the urge to be reactive. Instead, we must appeal to Christ, who can overcome it all. We must refuse to engage unless it's on our terms, by the power of the Spirit and completely in His will.[3]

An example worth looking at is the business world. Businesses that are trying to react to trends are typically striving to keep up. Consequently, they end up with stock that has suddenly become "outdated."

On the other hand, businesses that are proactive see the new trends coming and prepare for them. They have the opportunity of riding the trend longer. Also, they have a sense of how long the trend will last and prepare accordingly."

Are you following Christian trends? Looking for the latest and greatest preacher or program? The irony of this type of behavior is that we aren't necessarily following the Holy Spirit.

---

[3] Barry, John D., and Rebecca Kruyswijk. *Connect the Testaments: A One-Year Daily Devotional with Bible Reading Plan.* Bellingham, WA: Lexham Press, 2012. Print.

If the devil can't distract you through direct temptation, he will use gimmicks and new programs to take you away from following the Holy Spirit. Many good ideas have become financial nightmares for both Christian's and Churches.

Be the trend setter in your community. Through prayer and fasting, get a plan of action from God Himself. Don't be surprised when other people mimic you! There will always be someone who still looks for the latest and greatest trend!

In your personal life, be steady and on the lookout for the devil's tactics. With great boldness, advance the Kingdom of God, do great things for God, and He will bless you abundantly.

Live to Win

In the sports world, some coaches play to win while others play not to lose. What's the difference? Playing to win means staying aggressive and adding to the score; defending your lead means you put your effort into defense, thus allowing your opponent an opportunity to mount a stronger attack against you.

Dear Christian, pray to win, not just maintain. Amen.

6. Be Strong in the Lord

Ephesians 6:10 (NKJV) [10] Finally, my brethren, be strong in the Lord and in the power of His might.

Every true child of God soon learns that the Christian life is warfare. The hosts of Satan are committed to hinder and obstruct the work of Christ and to knock the individual soldier out of combat.[4]

Warfare is a way of life. You can't escape it. As Christians we realize that there is more at stake in life than our personal comfort and satisfaction. There are people engaged in the battle of their life. We need to come along side of them and fight on their behalf.

Through the weapons of our warfare, we can pull down strongholds, principalities and powers of darkness:

---

[4]William MacDonald and Arthur Farstad, *Believer's Bible Commentary: Old and New Testaments*, Eph 6:10 (Nashville: Thomas Nelson, 1997, c1995).

2 Corinthians 10:3–6 (NKJV) ³ For though we walk in the flesh, we do not war according to the flesh. ⁴ For the weapons of our warfare *are* not carnal but mighty in God for pulling down strongholds, ⁵ casting down arguments and every high thing that exalts itself against the knowledge of God, bringing every thought into captivity to the obedience of Christ, ⁶ and being ready to punish all disobedience when your obedience is fulfilled.

Our Strength is in the Lord

Are you strong in the Lord and the power of His might? Do you find that you can't do it on your own? Will power is not enough. Instead of trying to strengthen your willpower, you need to surrender your will to God. By dressing in the armor of God, you can protect yourself from the temptations and strong desires that pull at you.

When you are trying to overcome a life controlling habit, simply willing it to be won't last. Until the root of the addiction is dealt with, it will keep returning and bearing its fruit of control and destruction.

The key to overcoming an addiction is to deal with it through the power of God. You can't defeat the devil or destructive lifestyles with the power of the soul; you need God's help.

Satan wants you to fail. He will bombard you with negativity, doubts and fears. Satan will work through people who are weak and selfish. It doesn't matter if they attend Church or not. They can still be used to take you down.

Why would people who are close to you discourage you and try to get you to be mediocre like them? Because they want your failure to be their excuse for not trying; they are too lazy to seek after God's destiny for their lives. If you try and do succeed, they will be convicted.

Resisting Evil

There is no victory, no success, without resistance. You will be resisted and you must also resist.

> *Ephesians 6:13 (NKJV) [13] Therefore take up the whole armor of God, that you may be able to withstand in the evil day, and having done all, to stand.*

The word "withstand" has the meaning of taking a stand. It also means to stand with someone. In the context of warfare, we are actually taking a stand with God and resisting His enemies.

"But Pastor Bruce, I don't like conflict. I want it to be easy. Isn't faith supposed to make my life easier?" No! You need a reality check. The very faith you live by and claim for protection is the very thing that offends the devil the most. He can't stand faith!

> Hebrews 11:6 (NKJV) But without faith *it is* impossible to please *Him,* for he who comes to God must believe that He is, and *that* He is a rewarder of those who diligently seek Him.

If it is impossible to please God without faith, then faith has to be the very thing that the devil will attack. If God rewards you for diligently seeking Him, then expect resistance to diligence!

> *James 4:7 (NKJV) Therefore, submit to God. Resist the devil and he will flee from you.*

Have you ever taken an antihistamine when you have had a cold? It is the same Greek word used here for resist. In the same manner that you want your medicine to bring relief and healing, so it is with your faith. You use it and the word of God to forcefully stop the devil from fighting against you.

Face Challenges and Embrace Them

Satan hates Christians that face their challenges and embrace tribulation. His design in tribulation and persecution is for you to cut and run with your tail between your legs. Your failure is the devil's success. Don't help him!

There isn't a place of neutrality when it comes to warfare. You are either with God or against Him. If you are with God, then you can expect hostility from the devil and his servants.

There is an advantage for Christian's that embrace tribulation and persecution; they grow!

> *Romans 5:3-4 (NKJV) ³ and not only that, but we also glory in tribulations, knowing that tribulation produces perseverance; ⁴ and perseverance, character; and character, hope.*

You can't take a strong stand without perseverance; perseverance can't be built through doctrinal or theological studies. Perseverance comes through tribulation.

Another interesting revelation that comes from reading this particular passage is that character is a result of perseverance. The greatest reason for a lack of character in the Church today is an unwillingness to embrace tribulation, take a stand against the devil and to be counted for God.

Too many Christians are looking for deliverance from tribulation and not looking for deliverance through tribulation. Do you understand the difference? Tribulation can make you aware of what you need to change in your own life. Let it expose your weakness so that you can surrender it to Christ and grow.

The cure for hopelessness in your life is to develop strong Christian character; strong character comes from perseverance, and perseverance comes from embracing your tribulations.

7. Our Responsibility

1 Corinthians 15:58 (NKJV) [58] Therefore, my beloved brethren, be steadfast, immovable, always abounding in the work of the Lord, knowing that your labor is not in vain in the Lord.

A lot of people are moved by their emotions and do not know how to be led by the Holy Spirit. They evaluate life based on what they can see and how it makes them feel at the time.

I have encountered Christians who are "anointing junkies." They are looking for someone to impart a great anointing into them so they can become victorious and successful. After the meetings are done and life meets them with a vengeance, they collapse.

Instead of being discipled they look for another meeting or even another Church that is operating in the "anointing."

Where are the steadfast, immovable Christians that Paul refers to? They are few and far between. When you do find them, they bring refreshing into your life.

As a ministry leader, I pray for people to become stable and reliable. Gifts are important, but being able to count on you being there with your gift is even more important! When the chips are down, you need to be reliable and trustworthy.

Faith is not in Vain

The motive for steadfast living is that our faith is not in vain. Have you ever wondered if believing and holding on was somehow not worth it? It's in the darkest moments, the hardest time of a testing, when you feel the weakest and most vulnerable that God is bringing a breakthrough.

The ultimate trial of a Christian is undoubtedly facing death. Why do some Christian's just seem to face the possibility of death with joy in their heart and a gleam in their eye? They ***know*** that Jesus has conquered death, hell and the grave. Beyond death awaits a glorious meeting with Jesus and the Saints who have gone on before us.

Knowing that not even death has the final say, we can face the adversities of life with hope of the future promise of not only being in Heaven with Jesus, but also of the final resurrection when we are given new, glorified bodies.

Abounding in the Work of the Lord

Knowing that Jesus has conquered death and the grave not only motivates the believer to ethical, moral living; it is also a motivation to work.

Just believing is not enough for Christian's. We are saved by grace through faith and not of works, but we are saved unto good works (see Eph. 2:8-9). We have been given a commission by

Jesus Christ and that is to go, make disciples, baptize them and teach them how to live for Jesus.

Steadfast, immovable living and faithfulness to the task at hand require us to live in the present with the future clearly in view. Keep the present realities with all the suffering, anguish, disappointments, successes and great victories balanced with the future reality of not only Heaven, but also our ruling and reigning with Christ in His millennial reign on earth.

Don't Waver

Once you have made a decision to follow Christ, don't waver. Be bold and determined to finish strong. Don't falter in your thinking.

I once heard the story of a Kentucky politician. His hometown was a small village that had a few farms. The residents in the town were divided over the issue of raising chickens in the village limits.

Many of the citizens felt it should not be allowed, due to the smell and the noise. Others, however, felt that it was their right as Americans to be free enough to raise chickens if they wanted to.

On a visit to the village, the politician was confronted with this seeming dilemma. He was asked where he stood on the issue. His response was a classic. The politician responded by saying, "Well, some of my friends are for it, some of my friends are against it. As for me, well, I'm standing with my friends!"

As a Christian, you have to take a stand with God and not waver with popular opinion.

JESUS SAVES • JESUS HEALS • JESUS DELIVERS

I'm going to say a quick prayer for you. Lord, bless (FILL IN NAME) and his/her family with long and healthy lives. Jesus, make Yourself real to him/her and do a quick work in his/her heart. If (FILL IN NAME) has not received Jesus Christ as his/her Lord and Savior, I pray he/she will do so now.

(FILL IN NAME), if you would like to receive the gift that God has for you today, say this after me with your heart and lips out loud. Dear Lord Jesus, come into my heart. Forgive me of my sin. Wash me and cleanse me. Set me free. Jesus, thank You that You died for me. I believe that You are risen from the dead and that You're coming back again for me. Fill me with the Holy Spirit. Give me a passion for the lost, a hunger for the things of God and a holy boldness to preach the gospel of Jesus Christ. I'm saved; I'm born again, I'm forgiven and I'm on my way to Heaven because I have Jesus in my heart.

As a minister of the gospel of Jesus Christ, I tell you today that all of your sins are forgiven. Always remember to run to God and not from God because He loves you and has a great plan for your life.

[Invite them to your church and get follow up info: name, address, & phone number.]

Revival Ministries International
Please, register as a Soul Saving Station at revival.com/JoinS3 and log your soul count regularly.

THE GOSPEL SOUL-WINNING —SCRIPT—

Has anyone ever told you that God loves you and that He has a wonderful plan for your life? I have a real quick, but important question to ask you. If you were to die this very second, do you know for sure, beyond a shadow of a doubt, that you would go to Heaven? [If "Yes"— Great, why would you say "Yes"? (If they respond with anything but "I have Jesus in my heart" or something similar to that, PROCEED WITH SCRIPT) or "No" or "I hope so" PROCEED WITH SCRIPT.]

Let me quickly share with you what the Holy Bible reads. It reads "for all have sinned and come short of the glory of God" and "for the wages of sin is death, but the gift of God is eternal life through Jesus Christ our Lord". The Bible also reads, "For whosoever shall call upon the name of the Lord shall be saved". And you're a "whosoever" right? Of course you are; all of us are.

continued on reverse side—

8. Finish What You Start

Luke 14:28 (NKJV) [28] For which of you, intending to build a tower, does not sit down first and count the cost, whether he has enough to finish it—

Have you ever started something you weren't able to finish? While in High School, I was a member of the Cross-Country team. Looking back on that time, I have been able to see a lot of spiritual truths revealed. Every race seemed to have at least one "rabbit." He was the runner who took off in almost a sprint. By the time you finished the first quarter mile, he was far ahead. But, without fail, he would be caught by the rest of the pack by the one-mile mark, and most usually passed by them all. Sometimes, the rabbit didn't even finish.

The rabbit didn't know how to pace himself. He didn't realize what it would take to be able to finish well.

Time to Sprint

For the long-distance runner, the time to sprint is at the end of the race. Throughout the race, a steady pace has been kept, but now, it's time to pour everything you have left into the last stretch. The sprint to the finish is on. In the last stretch, I have personally experienced moving from the top ten into the top three finishers. I wasn't about to settle for anything less than a top five finish.

Now, life is like a long-distance race. Someday, your race will be finished. You will either make it to the finish line, or you will make it to the sidelines. Age isn't an excuse for tossing in the towel and limping to the finish line.

A lot of Christian's start out great. The serve, learn and grow. They show great potential and affect many people. But, when they get older, they give up. Why would they give up after serving for so many years and seeing the results of successful living? They failed to learn to stand in adversity.

You may be a theologian who is knowledgeable and worthy of being listened to. But, even with all of your knowledge, you will fail in the end if you don't learn how to stand in adversity.

A Warning from Paul

1 Corinthians 10:12 (NKJV) ¹² Therefore let him who thinks he stands take heed lest he fall.

Self-confidence will lead to a fall. There are many who take great pride in their personal abilities and their knowledge. How could they ever fall? It's when we begin thinking that way, that we are about to take a journey into failure.

You cannot play with fire and not have it affect you. You will ultimately have to deal with the harvest you get from self-indulgence and personal gratification.

Depend upon God and His strength. Realize that you are as just as capable of falling as the weakest Christian on earth. You really are not an exception because you are "anointed." I believe the greatest cause of ministry failure is due to people believing that God makes an exception for them because of what they do for the Church.

Repent of any self-centeredness and humble yourself in the sight of God or he will humble you in the sight of mankind.

9. Stand Firm; Stand Fast

Philippians 4:1 (NKJV) ¹ Therefore, my beloved and longed-for brethren, my joy and crown, so <u>stand fast in the Lord</u>, beloved.

Hold on to what you have received from the Lord. The devil wants to draw you into a battle where you end up compromising and forfeiting your reward. The Bible gives us ample warning to this effect. The Apostle John warned his readers of this:

2 John 8 (NKJV) ⁸ Look to yourselves, that we do not lose those things we worked for, but that we may receive a full reward.

Are you really willing to forfeit all that you have gained from Christ for a few momentary pleasures? Men and women today sacrifice their families, careers, homes and their reputations for pleasures that last for only a season. Drug addicts and alcoholics can't hold on to their possessions or relationships for long. Their selfishness that has gotten them into the mess they are in will control them and ultimately destroy them.

Selfishness will not allow you to evaluate your present decisions in the light of the future. It's all about gratification, instant gratification. As long as you only care about how you feel at the moment, you will live without any values and hope for future success.

Where Will You Be After the Smoke Has Cleared?

When the battle is done and the smoke has cleared, where will you be found standing? I want to be standing for Jesus. Though it may seem a narrow thing to do, it is a necessary thing. Many opportunities to satisfy our own desires will come our way. Will you put yourself first, or will you live for the will of God? Your reward lies in your faithfulness to Jesus and His ways.

Casting our Crowns

When it's all said and done, we will cast our crowns at the feet of Jesus, the One who made us able to compete and win.

> *Revelation 4:10 (NKJV) [10] the twenty-four elders fall down before Him who sits on the throne and worship Him who lives forever and ever, and cast their crowns before the throne, saying: [11] "You are worthy, O Lord, To receive glory and honor and power; For You created all things, And by Your will they exist and were created."*

Will you cast your crown at the feet of Jesus, or will you cast it at the feet of the world now? When you give up, you are actually casting away your crown.

When the Saints in Heaven are casting their crowns at the feet of Jesus, it symbolizes a willing submission and subjection to the superiority and supremacy of Jesus. Therefore, if we cast away our crowns at the feet of the world, we are submitting ourselves to the powers of this world and its rulers.

There Is More to Come

There is so much more yet to come. We are in training to rule and reign with Jesus in His kingdom. As faithful followers of Jesus, we will be given positions of responsibility in His government. We will serve with men like David, Paul, Peter, James, and many other faithful believers that have gone on before us.

Learn to Stand Under Pressure

1 Corinthians 9:25-27 (NKJV) [25] And everyone who competes for the prize is temperate in all things. Now they do it to obtain a perishable crown, but we for an imperishable crown. [26] Therefore I run thus: not with uncertainty. Thus I fight not as one who beats the air. [27] But I discipline my body and bring it into subjection, lest, when I have preached to others, I myself should become disqualified.

The word of the hour is "temperance." What is it? It is control over sensual desires. The senses are given to our body so that we can be aware of the world around us. However, when we use them only to gratify the flesh, it becomes ungodly. By practicing temperance, I am bringing my body under the control of what the Spirit desires me to use it for.

Our bodies are to be surrendered to the use of the Holy Spirit so that He can express Himself in and through us. Temperance is required by us to allow Him the freedom to flow. If you want to be used mightily in the Gifts of the Spirit, then you must train your body to be obedient to the desires of the Holy Spirit.

The temperance I am referring to is not a matter of will power; it is listed in the fruit of the Spirit. Hence, you cannot produce it on your own but only through yielding to the Holy Spirit.

My part in the development of the fruit of the Spirit is yielding, resisting and crucifying the flesh. As a person, I must resist the inclinations of the flesh and put them to death; by so doing I am able to receive the power of the Lord in order to stand.

(Galatians 5:24 (NKJV) [24] and those who are Christ's have crucified the flesh with its passions and desires.

Through Christ the domination of the flesh was broken. Even though we still have a sinful nature to deal with, it does not control and dominate us like it did before we were born again. I deal with my flesh by denying it the gratification that it seeks.

The True Strength of a Preacher

The strength of a preacher is not found in how many souls he can get saved; his strength is in being able to stand in adversity, and while under persecution, pressure and temptation, not yielding to the flesh.

How well are you managing your life? Don't cast away your crown for worldly fame, sex outside of the boundaries of marriage, drugs or alcohol. These are all temporary elements that will ultimately destroy you.

Put on the armor of God and take a stand for the rest of your life.

Dr. Bruce Fletcher is Pastor of Bethel Christian Church, West Hartford, CT. He is also the founder and President of ACTS Ministries International, Inc.

To find out more about ACTS and Dr. Bruce, write us at:

ACTS Ministries International

106 South St

West Hartford, CT 06110

Made in the USA
Monee, IL
17 July 2020